These notes refer to the Prisons (Interference with Wireless Telegraphy) Bill as introduced in the House of Commons on 20 June 2012 [Bill 15]

PRISONS (INTERFERENCE WITH WIRELESS TELEGRAPHY) BILL

EXPLANATORY NOTES

INTRODUCTION

1. These Explanatory Notes relate to the Prisons (Interference with Wireless Telegraphy) Bill as introduced in the House of Commons on 20 June 2012. They have been provided by the Ministry of Justice, with the consent of Sir Paul Beresford MP, the Member in charge of the Bill, in order to assist the reader of the Bill and to help inform debate on it. They do not form part of the Bill and have not been endorsed by Parliament.

2. The Notes need to be read in conjunction with the Bill. They are not, and are not meant to be, a comprehensive description of the Bill. So where a clause or part of a clause does not seem to require any explanation or comment, none is given.

SUMMARY

3. The Bill makes provision for the Secretary of State in respect of England and Wales, and the Scottish Ministers in respect of Scotland, to authorise governors and directors of relevant institutions to interfere with wireless telegraphy in order to prevent the use of electronic communications devices (including mobile telephones) in, or detect or investigate the use of such devices within, relevant institutions. In England and Wales 'relevant institutions' are prisons, young offender institutions and secure training centres. In Scotland, 'relevant institutions' are prisons and young offenders institutions. The Bill provides that the detection or investigation of the use of such devices may be carried out by collecting 'traffic data' in relation to a communication. The definition of traffic data is discussed in paragraph 15 of these Notes.

*These notes refer to the Prisons (Interference with Wireless Telegraphy) Bill
as introduced in the House of Commons on 20 June 2012 [Bill 15]*

4. The Bill makes provision for safeguards in order to ensure that, in particular, any undue interference with wireless telegraphy outside of the relevant institution is limited. The Bill also provides safeguards regarding the retention and disclosure of information obtained in the exercise of powers under an authorisation. In particular, the Bill provides that any information obtained by detecting or investigating the use of electronic communication devices in relevant institutions must be destroyed no later than three months after it was obtained unless the governor or director of the relevant institution authorises its continued retention as being necessary and proportionate on specified grounds. The information obtained may not be disclosed other than to specified persons unless such disclosure is considered as being necessary and proportionate on specified grounds.

BACKGROUND

5. The presence of wireless telegraphy devices, in particular, illicit mobile telephones presents serious risks to the security of prisons and the other institutions to which the Bill applies, as well as to the safety of the public. Mobile telephones are used for a range of criminal purposes in these institutions, including commissioning serious violence, harassing victims and continuing involvement in extremist networks, organised crime and gang activity. Access to mobile telephones is also strongly associated with drug supply, violence and bullying. The 2008 Blakey report 'Disrupting the Supply of Drugs into Prisons'[1] identified the availability of mobile telephones as key to the smuggling of drugs into prisons.

6. In England and Wales the criminal law already prohibits the taking into or use of electronic communications devices, including mobile telephones, within relevant institutions. In England and Wales, sections 40A, 40C and 40D of the Prison Act 1952 provide that it is an offence to convey an electronic communications device, or component part, into or out of a prison, or to transmit sounds or images from within a prison without authorisation or to possess a mobile telephone in prison without authorisation. These offences, which also apply to secure training centres and young offender institutions, carry a penalty of up to two years' imprisonment and/or an unlimited fine. It is also a disciplinary offence to possess a mobile telephone within a prison or young offender institution.

7. In Scotland section 41ZA of the Prisons (Scotland) Act 1989 provides that it is an offence to possess, or give to a prisoner in prison, or use, without authorisation or outside of the designated area of the prison, a personal communication device such as a mobile telephone or any other portable electronic device capable of transmitting or receiving a communication. Section 41 of the Prisons (Scotland) Act 1989 provides that it is unlawful to bring a personal communication device such as a mobile telephone into a prison or a young offenders institution. It is also a disciplinary

---

[1] The Blakey Review, July 2008

These notes refer to the Prisons (Interference with Wireless Telegraphy) Bill as introduced in the House of Commons on 20 June 2012 [Bill 15]

offence to possess a personal communication device such as a mobile telephone in a prison or young offenders institution.

8. The problems posed by mobile phones in prisons were recently identified in the Home Office national drug strategy 2010[2], a 2010 Ministry of Justice green paper[3] and the Home Office organised crime strategy[4].

9. In Scotland, a Strategy for Tackling Serious Organised Crime entitled "Letting Our Communities Flourish" was published in 2009 on behalf of the Serious and Organised Crime Taskforce. This includes Scottish Government, ACPO(S), the Crown Office and Procurator Fiscal Service, the Scottish Crime and Drug Enforcement Agency, the Scottish Prison Service and HMRC.

10. The provisions of the Bill are designed to create a clear and transparent legal basis on which signal interference equipment can be used within relevant institutions to enable the authorities to find mobile telephones and to disrupt, by means of signal interference equipment, the use of those telephones that cannot be found.

TERRITORIAL EXTENT AND APPLICATION

11. The Bill extends to England, Wales and Scotland. In relation to Wales the provisions relate to non-devolved matters. In relation to Scotland wireless telegraphy is a reserved matter. However clauses 1 and 2 affect the executive competence of Scottish Ministers in relation to the operation of prisons. The Sewel Convention provides that Westminster will not normally legislate with regard to devolved matters in Scotland without the consent of the Scottish Parliament. Insofar as the provisions in the Bill confer powers on the Scottish Ministers, the Scottish Government has provided confirmation, in principle, that it will seek the necessary Legislative Consent Motion. If amendments are made to the Bill that trigger a requirement for a Legislative Consent Motion, the consent of the Scottish Parliament will be sought for them.

COMMENTARY ON CLAUSES

Clause 1: Interference with wireless telegraphy in prisons etc.

12. Clause 1 provides for the authorisation of interference with wireless telegraphy for the purpose of preventing, detecting or investigating the use of electronic communications devices (including mobile telephones) within prisons and similar institutions.

---

[2] "Reducing demand, restricting supply, building recovery: supporting people to live a drug-free life" - www.homeoffice.gov.uk/publications/alcohol-drugs/drugs/drug-strategy/drug-strategy-2010
[3] "Breaking the Cycle: Effective Punishment, Rehabilitation and Sentencing of Offenders" - www.justice.gov.uk/consultations/docs/breaking-the-cycle.pdf
[4] "Local to Global: Reducing the Risk from Organised Crime" - www.homeoffice.gov.uk/publications/crime

*These notes refer to the Prisons (Interference with Wireless Telegraphy) Bill
as introduced in the House of Commons on 20 June 2012 [Bill 15]*

13. *Subsection* (1) provides that the appropriate national authority, which is defined in clause 4(1) as the Secretary of State in relation to an institution in England and Wales and the Scottish Ministers in relation to an institution in Scotland, may authorise the person in charge of a relevant institution to interfere with wireless telegraphy. 'Relevant institution' means a prison in England, Wales or Scotland, a young offender institution in England or Wales, a young offenders institution in Scotland, and a secure training centre in England or Wales (clause 4(1)). The person in charge of a relevant institution is, in relation to England and Wales, the governor of a prison, young offender institution, or secure training centre or, where the prison, young offender institution or secure training centre has been contracted out, the director of that institution (clause 4(2)). In relation to Scotland, the person in charge of a relevant institution is the governor or, where the institution has been contracted out, the director of a prison or young offenders institution (clause 4(2)).

14. *Subsection* (2) provides that an interference with wireless telegraphy authorised under *subsection* (1) may be carried out only for the purpose of preventing the use within the institution of an item specified in *subsection* (3) or detecting or investigating the use of such an item. The specified items are devices capable of transmitting or receiving images, sounds or information by electronic communications. This includes mobile telephones as well as other devices which are capable of accessing the internet or are otherwise capable of sending or receiving data. The specified items also include any component part or article designed or adapted for use with electronic communications devices.

15. *Subsection* (4) provides that the interference with wireless telegraphy that may be carried out in accordance with *subsection* (2) for the purpose of detecting or investigating the use of the specified items is for the collection of traffic data in relation to an electronic communication. The term 'traffic data' is defined in clause 4(4) and (5) and includes data which is comprised in, attached to or logically associated with an electronic communication and which identifies the person or apparatus or location to or from which the communication is transmitted; identifies apparatus through which the communication is transmitted; or identifies the time at which an event relating to the communication occurs. It does not include the content of the communication.

16. *Subsection* (5) and (6) makes lawful for all purposes:

> a) an interference with wireless telegraphy that is authorised under *subsection* (1) and is carried out in accordance with *subsection* (2) and any direction given under clause 2;
> b) the retention, use or disclosure of any traffic data, collected as a result of any such interference with wireless telegraphy, which is carried out in accordance with the Act.

17. *Subsection* (7) provides that section 8(1) of the Wireless Telegraphy Act 2006 does not apply in relation to anything done for the purposes of carrying out an interference

with wireless telegraphy authorised by this clause. The effect of this is that a licence granted by the Office of Communications (OFCOM) is not required for the installation and use of equipment to interfere with wireless telegraphy in accordance with clause 1 of the Bill.

18. Any authorisation under clause 1 must be in writing (*subsection* (8)).

Clause 2: Safeguards

19. This clause sets out the safeguards which apply in relation to the granting of authorisations under clause 1.

20. *Subsection* (1) provides that, before an authorisation can be granted, the appropriate national authority must be satisfied that the equipment that will be used as a result of the authorisation is fit for purpose. In addition, under *subsection* (2) where an authorisation is granted, the relevant national authority must inform OFCOM of the authorisation.

21. *Subsection* (3) requires a person in charge of a relevant institution who is authorised to interfere with wireless telegraphy under section 1 to act in accordance with any directions given under this clause. In accordance with *subsection* (4), certain directions must be given whenever an authorisation is granted, including directions regarding requirements to provide information to OFCOM; and about the circumstances in which the use of the equipment under the authorisation must be modified or discontinued (and, in particular, directions aimed at ensuring that the authorised interference will not result in disproportionate interference with wireless telegraphy outside the relevant institution). All directions must be given in writing (*subsection* (6)).

Clause 3: Retention and disclosure of information obtained under section 1

22. This clause governs the retention and disclosure of information obtained in accordance with an authorisation under clause 1 of the Bill. This information will be traffic data described in paragraph 15 above.

23. Under *subsection* (1), the information must be destroyed no later than 3 months after it was obtained unless the person in charge of the relevant institution has authorised its retention. Further, under *subsection* (2) retention may only be authorised if the person in charge of a relevant institution is satisfied that retention is necessary on the grounds set out in *subsection* (8) and is proportionate to that purpose.

24. *Subsection* (3) provides that where information is retained under *subsection* (1), the person in charge of the relevant institution is under an obligation to review whether its retention continues to be justified. Such reviews must take place at least every 3 months. Where the person in charge of the relevant institution is not satisfied that retention of the information remains justified the information must be destroyed (*subsection* (4)).

25. *Subsection* (5) provides that information obtained to detect and investigate the use of the items specified in clause 1(3) may be disclosed to an officer or an authorised employee of the relevant institution; or the Secretary of State or the Scottish Ministers if the relevant institution is in Scotland, unless the person in charge of the relevant institution has authorised the disclosure. *Subsection* (6) provides that the information may not be disclosed to any other person unless the person in charge of a relevant institution has authorised that disclosure. Such authorisation may be given only where the disclosure is necessary on the grounds set out in *subsection* (8) and is proportionate to that purpose (*subsection* (7))..

26. The grounds referred to in *subsection* (2) and *subsection* (7) are set out in *subsection* (8). These are: the interests of national security, the prevention, detection, investigation or prosecution of crime, the interests of public safety, securing or maintaining security or good order and discipline in the relevant institution, and the protection of health or morals.

COMMENCEMENT

27. Clause 5(2) provides that the substantive provisions of the Bill will be brought into force in England and Wales by means of commencement order made by the Secretary of State and, in relation to Scotland, by a commencement order made by the Scottish Ministers.

FINANCIAL EFFECTS OF THE BILL

28. The Bill will impose no financial obligations on the public sector. However, the Bill will make it possible for deployments of signal denial equipment to take place, where the appropriate national authority considers that the benefits of such deployment provide suitable justification for the costs.

EFFECTS OF THE BILL ON PUBLIC SECTOR MANPOWER

29. The provisions of the Bill are not expected to have an impact on public sector manpower. As above, the Bill will impose no obligations on the appropriate national authority to undertake additional activity.

SUMMARY OF IMPACT ASSESSMENTS

30. As the proposed policy changes are unlikely to lead to costs or savings for business, public or civil society organisation, regulators or consumers, a full impact assessment has not been completed.

*These notes refer to the Prisons (Interference with Wireless Telegraphy) Bill
as introduced in the House of Commons on 20 June 2012 [Bill 15]*

31. An initial screening has been undertaken by the Ministry of Justice which confirmed that a full Equality Impact Assessment is not necessary. The provisions in the Bill will impact upon all prisoners using illicit electronic communications devices such as mobile phones in a relevant institution equally.

PRISONS (INTERFERENCE WITH WIRELESS TELEGRAPHY) BILL

EXPLANATORY NOTES

These notes refer to the Prisons (Interference with Wireless Telegraphy) Bill as introduced in the House of Commons on 20 June 2012 [Bill 15]

Ordered, by The House of Commons,
to be Printed, 28 June 2012.

© Parliamentary copyright House of Commons 2012
This publication may be reproduced under the terms of the Parliamentary Click-Use Licence, available online through The National Archives website at
www.nationalarchives.gov.uk/information-management/our-services/parliamentary-licence-information.htm
Enquiries to The National Archives, Kew, Richmond, Surrey, TW9 4DU;
email: psi@nationalarchives.gsi.gov.uk

PUBLISHED BY AUTHORITY OF THE HOUSE OF COMMONS
LONDON — THE STATIONERY OFFICE LIMITED
Printed in the United Kingdom by The Stationery Office Limited
£2.00

Bill 15—EN   (21951)   55/2